The Marvelous Music Machine

A Story of the Piano

by Mary Blocksma

illustrated by Mischa Richter

Prentice-Hall, Inc.
Englewood Cliffs, New Jersey

Printed in the United States of America   ·J

Prentice-Hall International, Inc., London
Prentice-Hall of Australia, Pty. Ltd., Sydney
Prentice-Hall of Canada, Ltd., Toronto
Prentice-Hall of India Private Ltd., New Delhi
Prentice-Hall of Japan, Inc., Tokyo
Prentice-Hall of Southeast Asia Pte. Ltd., Singapore
Whitehall Books Limited, Wellington, New Zealand
Editora Prentice-Hall do Brasil LTDA., Rio de Janeiro

10 9 8 7 6 5 4 3 2 1

Library of Congress Cataloging in Publication Data

Blocksma, Mary.
  The marvelous music machine.

  Summary: A history of the piano explaining how it is
made, how it works, and many unusual facts about the
instrument.

  1. Piano—History—Juvenile literature. [1. Piano—
History] I. Richter, Mischa, 1910– ill. II. Title.
ML650.B55   1984   786.2'1'09   84-4892
ISBN 0-13-559410-3

To my mother,
Ruth Blocksma,
who loves kids and pianos

Acknowledgments

I wish to express grateful appreciation to the many individuals who have helped me in the writing of this book. They include piano teachers Brenda Turnbull and Julia Blocksma, and piano technicians Trudy Ferguson and L. Sue Bender.

Special thanks are due to John Steinway, Horace Comstock, Joseph J. Pramberger, and all the wonderful people at Steinway & Sons, who gave me much helpful information.

I am also indebted to piano authority Bob Pierce, pianist John Cobb, piano technician Lucille Rains, and to the many piano teachers and piano tuners who answered my questions.

Special appreciation goes to the gifted illustrator Mischa Richter, to my editors, and to my family who so patiently assisted me.

The Marvelous Music Machine

The piano is one of the biggest, most amazing, most popular music machines ever invented. There are probably 30 million pianos in the United States today, and over a million new and used pianos are sold every year. There are at least 50,000 piano teachers, who keep busy teaching their hundreds of thousands of students.

Despite those big numbers, most piano players know surprisingly little about the piano. To them, the piano is a marvelous MYSTERY machine. Maybe they have never really LOOKED at a piano—or IN one.

In this book, you will do both. In fact, by the time you finish, you might be almost an expert.

What's Grand About a Grand Piano?

Today's biggest piano is called a concert grand. It has three legs, a lid that flips up, and a gigantic body. Most often it is dressed in a thin, skin-tight layer of African wood and painted a gleaming black. A concert grand is so big that it won't fit in most livingrooms. It usually stars on the stage of a concert hall.

What else is grand about a concert grand piano?

It's heavy!

The concert grand is the heavyweight of the piano family. It weighs in at about 1,000 pounds—that's half a ton! To help ordinary people move it around, it usually has rollers for feet.

It's long!

If you stood a concert grand on its keyboard end, the other end would probably bust through your ceiling. The concert grand piano can be nine feet long, or more.

It's got a lot of guts!

If you could take a concert grand apart, you would pile up 12,000 pieces. It takes a piano company more than a year to build a concert grand piano. Nearly 400 people help put all those parts together.

It's strong!

The strings in a concert grand piano are stretched so tightly that it would take the strength of eleven elephants to hold them. But with a herd of elephants on stage, no one would hear the concert, so an iron frame holds the strings instead. The strings of a concert grand put 43,000 pounds of pressure on the iron frame.

It's talented!

It took hundreds of years to invent a keyboard instrument that could play both loudly and softly. *Pianoforte* is the piano's full name. In Italian, *piano* means soft and *forte* means loud.

The piano can also sound several notes at once. Think about it—most instruments can only play one note at a time. Playing the piano is much like playing several instruments at once. It makes you wonder how the piano does it!

The Piano Makes Good Vibrations

All sound begins with the shivers. These shivers are called *sound vibrations*. Sound vibrations move the air in waves. When the waves reach you, they tickle your eardrums, making them vibrate, too. That's when you hear sound.

But how do the vibrations begin? If you touch your fingers to your throat while you talk, you can feel your vocal cords vibrate. You make them shiver by forcing air past them. Some instruments, like the trumpet, make sound this way, too. You blow air through them to begin the vibrations.

The piano, however, is a both a *percussion* and a *string* instrument. It works more like a drum—instead of air, an object hits the strings to start the vibrations. If you have a piano, touch the side of it with one hand while you play some low notes with the other. You can actually FEEL the whole piano vibrating.

It all begins with the *keyboard*.

The Keyboard

The 88 keys on the piano's keyboard are a kind of control panel. They are much longer than you might think, since you can only see part of them. In even the smallest pianos, each key is about as long as your forearm, from your elbow to your fingertips. The white keys are made of wood and covered with a thin layer of plastic. The black keys are solid plastic.

KEY COVER-UP

It was once hard to find good materials to cover piano keys. Cattlebone didn't polish very well, and sea shells (called mother-of-pearl) cracked. So for many years, the most popular key covers were made from elephant tusks—ivory.

So many elephants were killed for their valuable tusks that they were in danger of becoming extinct. Now laws have been passed to protect the elephants, and raw ivory can no longer be brought into the United States.

Today, piano keys are made of high-grade plastic, which most pianists like better than ivory. Ivory gets brittle and yellow with age, as teeth tend to do. But plastic keys stay hard and smooth and white for a piano's lifetime.

KEYBOARD CATASTROPHES!

Some piano builders tried to make the piano easier to play by changing the keyboard. One even succeeded. The Janko keyboard, shown below, was actually better and faster than the traditional keyboard. Pianists didn't want to learn the piano all over again, though, so it never caught on.

The *half-circle keyboard* was made so children could more easily reach the keys.

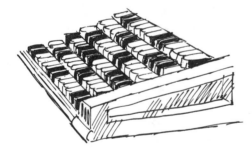

The Janko keyboard looked like a typewriter, with several rows of square keys.

The perpendicular piano was invented in 1878. Two keyboards sat on end, so a singer could stand and play at the same time.

The Action

When someone presses a piano key, the piano leaps into action. This is when most people say, "How mysterious!" and go on playing. It isn't really mysterious, though, if you take the piano apart. Only an expert should try this, so Tina, a piano tuner, will do it for you.

Tina begins by taking off the piano's *top front panel* (the vertical flat piece above the keyboard), the *music desk* (where you put the music when you're playing), and the *fall board* (the hinged wood piece that covers the keys). And there it is—the ACTION!

That long, orderly row of parts you see is called "the action" because those parts ACT on the piano's strings to start them vibrating. Since there are 88 keys, there are also 88 action sets, one for each key. And each action set— sometimes called "clever levers"—has a *hammer* (to start vibrations), a *damper* (to stop vibrations), and *check parts* (to make sure that everything is timed just right).

The Hammer

The hammer really begins the piano's sound. When Tina presses a key, the pear-shaped piece leaps forward and bounces off the strings. This starts the strings vibrating. The hammer waits close to the strings until Tina lets the key up; then it returns to its resting place.

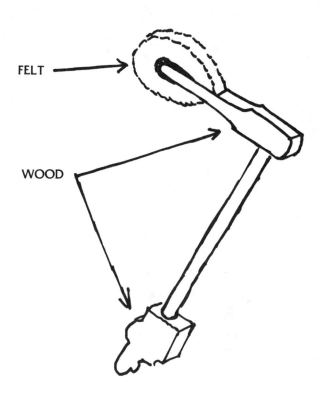

FELT

WOOD

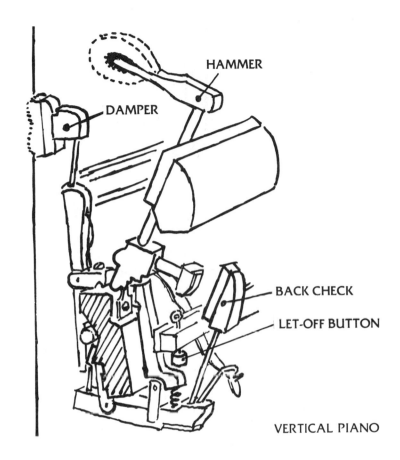

HAMMER

DAMPER

BACK CHECK

LET-OFF BUTTON

VERTICAL PIANO

The Check Parts

The check parts control the way the hammer moves. The *let-off button* makes sure that the hammer hits the string hard enough to bounce away. Without this button, the hammer might just lie against the strings, stopping the vibrations.

The back check stops the hammer from hitting the string twice. It holds the hammer close to the string until the key is released.

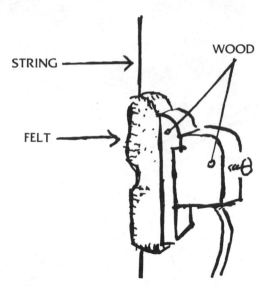

STRING

WOOD

FELT

The Damper

The damper is a soft sound-blocker made of felt. It rests against the strings until Tina presses the key. Then, as the hammer leaps toward the strings, the damper moves *away* from the strings. The strings can vibrate until Tina's finger moves off the key. Then the damper falls back and stops the sound.

To see how the hammer, the check parts, and the damper work, look at the drawing on pages 22–23.

The Pedals

The pedals, like the keyboard, are part of the player's control panel. You work these controls with your feet.

Every piano has at least two pedals. Each pedal is connected to a different part of the action.

The *soft pedal* on the left is connected to the hammer bar. When the pedal is pushed, the bar moves the hammers closer to the strings. When the hammers don't have so far to go, they hit the strings more gently and the sound they make is softer.

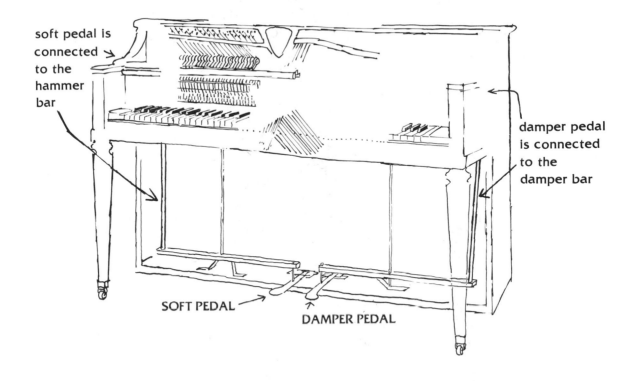

soft pedal is connected to the hammer bar

damper pedal is connected to the damper bar

SOFT PEDAL

DAMPER PEDAL

The *damper pedal*, sometimes called the sustaining pedal, is connected to the *dampers*. It is the one on the right. When Tina steps on the damper pedal, its rod pushes all the dampers away from the strings. The notes she plays keep sounding, even if she takes her hands off the keys. But when Tina takes her foot off the pedal, the dampers fall back against the strings. That stops the sound.

KNEE PEDALS

Before pianos had foot pedals, they sometimes came with "pedals" that could be pushed sideways by the player's knees. Some sewing machines still have knee controls very much like these.

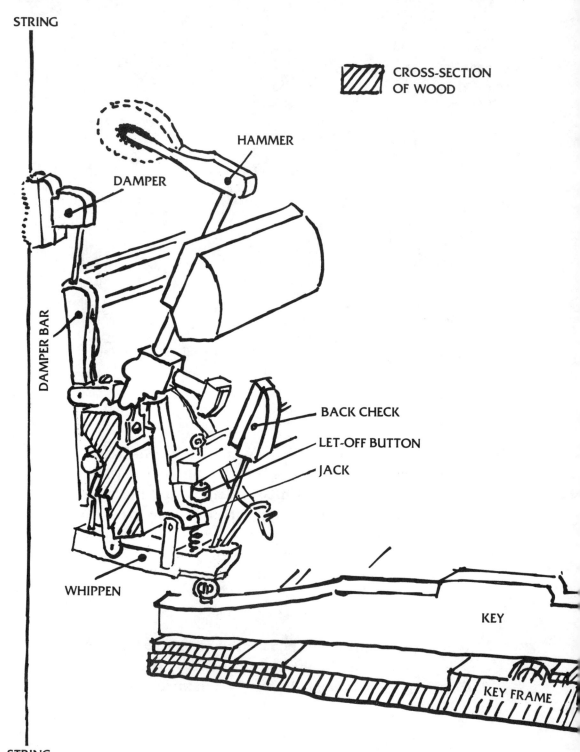

STRING

CROSS-SECTION OF WOOD

HAMMER

DAMPER

DAMPER BAR

BACK CHECK

LET-OFF BUTTON

JACK

WHIPPEN

KEY

KEY FRAME

STRING

How the Action Works

When you press a piano key, this is what happens:

The hammer hits the string.
1. The *key*, when pushed down, pushes the *whippen* up.
2. The *whippen* kicks the *jack* up.
3. The *jack* throws the hammer forward to hit the *string*.

The damper lets the string sound.
4. The *whippen* pushes the bottom of the *damper bar* toward the string.
5. The *damper* at the top of the bar is thrown away from the string so the string can vibrate. (When the key is let go, the damper moves back against the string and stops the sound.)

The checks control the movement of the hammer.
The check parts—the *let-off button* and the *back check*—stop the hammer from resting against the string or hitting it more than once. The action illustrated is for a vertical piano. The action looks different in a grand piano.

The Strings

Tina lifts out the entire action in one big piece. Now you can see the strings behind the action.

Piano strings are made of steel wire. Each string is tuned to a specific *pitch*.

The *pitch* of a note is how high or low the note sounds. The faster a string vibrates, the higher the note will be. The slower it vibrates, the lower the note. The speed of the vibrations—and therefore the pitch of the note—depends on the string's *thickness, length,* and *tension.*

STRANGE STRINGS

All kinds of materials have been tried for piano strings—gold, silver, glass, even silk. Today's steel strings work best.

KEYBOARD FOR A CAT?

A cat's keyboard would be bigger, not smaller, than ours. Cats can hear sounds that vibrate at 65,000 times per second! The highest sound that humans can hear vibrates at 20,000 times per second. So if cats could play the piano, they could use a keyboard three times the size of ours!

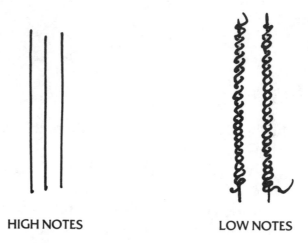

HIGH NOTES   **LOW NOTES**

Thickness

Thin wires vibrate faster than thick wires. So the high notes, which must vibrate very fast, have thin strings. Strings for the low notes, which vibrate more slowly, are thick. Copper wire is wrapped around the lowest strings to make them thicker.

Length

Short wires vibrate faster than long wires. So the high notes have short strings—strings only as long as your little finger make the highest notes. The lowest notes have the longest strings.

This explains why the piano wires are strung at an angle. This *cross-stringing* lets the low strings be longer than if they were straight up and down.

Tension

A wire's tension is its tightness. Tightly strung wires vibrate faster than loose wires. The high notes are made by tighter strings than the lower notes.

A piano has between 240 and 253 strings. Since there are only 88 keys, why so many strings? The answer to that has to do with *volume*, or loudness.

Most notes on the piano need extra strings because the wires are too short and thin to make much sound by themselves. More wires make the sound louder. The number of strings given each note is not the same in all pianos. In many, however, the top 62 notes have three strings each. The next 18 notes have two strings, and the bottom eight notes have one.

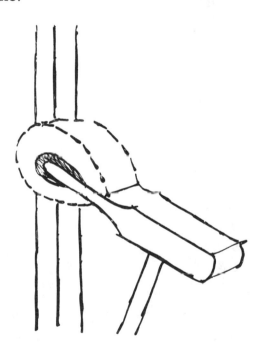

HOW IS A PIANO LIKE A MOTORCYCLE?

In Japan, the cast-iron frames for Yamaha pianos and the engine cases for Yamaha motorcycles are made in the same factory.

How to string a piano

It takes a strong, cast-iron *frame* to hold piano strings. Three *pins*—thick metal pegs—hold each string in place.

The string starts at the *tuning pin*. The tuning pin goes through the frame and screws into a piece of wood behind it, called the *pin block*.

The string's next stop is the *bridge pin*, which holds it to another piece of wood called the *bridge*. The other end of the string is fastened to the frame with a *hitch pin*.

The hammer hits the string between the tuning pin and the bridge pin. This part of the string is called its *speaking length*.

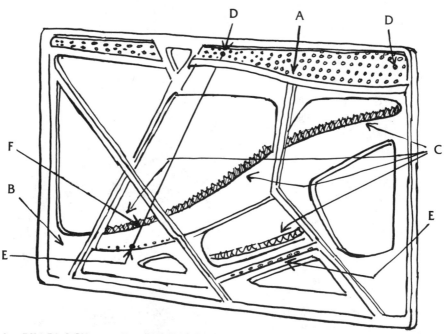

A. PIN BLOCK   D. TUNING PIN

B. FRAME   E. HITCH PIN

C. BRIDGES   F. BRIDGE PIN

The Resonator

The sound a string makes is not very loud. The piano has a *resonator*, or sound-builder, to make the music louder.

This resonator in the piano is called the *sounding board*.

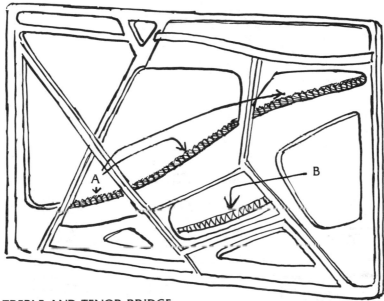

A. TREBLE AND TENOR BRIDGE

B. BASS BRIDGE

The Bridges

A string on the piano is stretched tightly across a piece of wood called a bridge. Every piano has two bridges, one for the low notes and a longer one for the higher notes. When the string vibrates, the bridge vibrates, too. Its job is to pass these vibrations on to the *sounding board*.

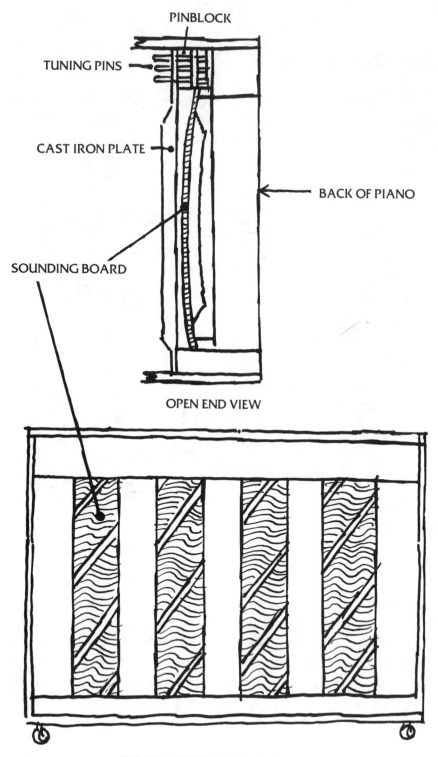

PINBLOCK

TUNING PINS

CAST IRON PLATE

BACK OF PIANO

SOUNDING BOARD

OPEN END VIEW

TYPICAL VERTICAL PIANO BACK

The Sounding Board

The bridges are attached to a big sheet of wood at the back of the piano, called the *sounding board*. The vibrations made by the strings travel through the bridge to the sounding board, which vibrates, too. The sounding board has a wide surface area. When it vibrates, it moves more air than a string can by itself. When more air moves, the sound gets louder.

The sounding board is hard to reach. If you could knock on it, though, it would sound like a big bass drum. It is shaped so that its center is thicker than its sides and the grains in the wood run like stripes in the same direction. The vibrations bounce off the sounding board like a child jumping on a trampoline. Only the vibrations are carried in many different directions at once, forming complex patterns.

SPRUCING UP THE SOUNDING BOARD

The Steinway & Sons piano factory makes sounding boards from special spruce trees that come from northern Alaska. The trees are 300 to 400 years old and measure 9 to 14 feet across!

PLUG YOUR EARS!

The Steinway piano factory uses a torture machine to loosen up the action on a newly built piano. Eighty-eight felt-covered, steel fingers come down 10,000 times on all the keys at once. Imagine the noise!

SEVEN KINDS OF WOOD!

Steinway uses many kinds of wood in pianos—in fact, the pianos are 80% wood. Here are some things the different woods are used for:

MAPLE—for the rim, bridge, action parts, pinblock
SPRUCE—for the sounding board
BIRCH—for the hammers
ROSEWOOD—for parts of the action
SUGAR PINE—for the keys
MAHOGANY—for the veneer, or outside finish
WALNUT—also for the veneer

THE WELL-TRAVELED PIANO

The materials used in pianos come from all over the world. Though not all piano companies get their materials from the same places, here is where the Steinway Piano Company gets theirs:

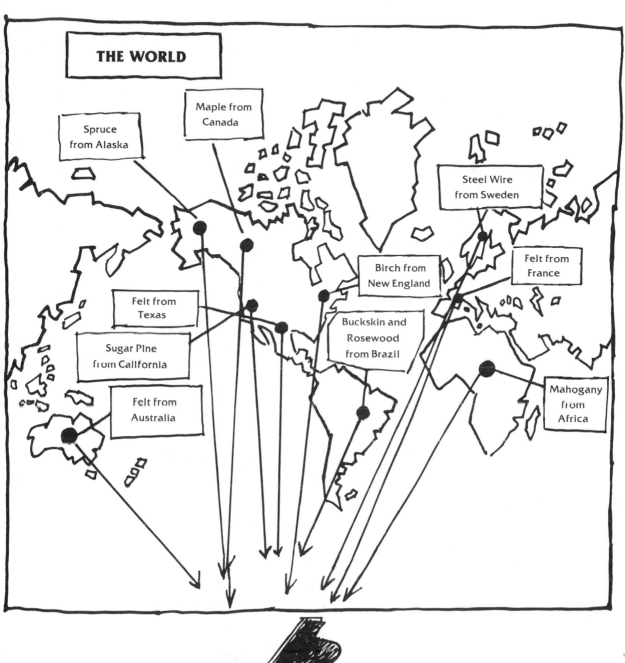

THE WORLD

Spruce from Alaska

Maple from Canada

Steel Wire from Sweden

Birch from New England

Felt from France

Felt from Texas

Sugar Pine from California

Buckskin and Rosewood from Brazil

Felt from Australia

Mahogany from Africa

The Piano was a Slow Grower

The marvelous music machine as you know it was not invented by just one person. It took nearly 2,250 years to build the first real piano, and thousands of people have worked on it. Many spent their entire lives trying to improve it.

The piano was not a beautiful baby.

The Monochord

The first instrument that was anything like a piano was a one-pound, one-string weakling called the *monochord*. The monochord, which appeared about 2,500 years ago, soon became the pop instrument of ancient Greece and Rome.

People played the monochord by pressing the string down at one end and plucking it at the other end. By pressing the string in different places, they could play a tune.

The monochord was such a simple instrument that folks fooled around with it to make it better. After about 2,000 years of fooling, it grew into an instrument called the *clavichord*.

The Clavichord

Instead of just one string, the clavichord had many tightly strung strings, each tuned to a different note. But the really different part of the clavichord was a new invention—keys. Players no longer had to pluck the strings with their fingers. Instead, when a player pressed one end of a key, a brass strip fastened to the other end would hit a string. Then the note would sound.

The clavichord was an amazing invention, but there were complaints about it. Its tinkling sound was so soft that it could hardly be heard. A whistle would drown out the music completely! So a new instrument was invented to correct that problem.

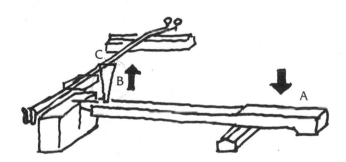

Clavichord Action

When the key (A) is pressed down, the brass blade or tangent (B) strikes a pair of strings (C), making them vibrate. The tangent stays against the strings until the key is let go.

The Harpsichord

It took instrument builders about 100 years to make the clavichord louder. To do it, they used quills—the hard stems of feathers—instead of brass strips. They called their new instruments *harpsichords*. When a harpsichord key was pressed, a quill plucked the string instead of hitting it.

The harpsichord was much louder than the clavichord. It was so loud, in fact, that people complained about it. The harpsichord couldn't play softly at all. The instrument makers tried all sorts of tricks to fix this. Some put in extra keyboards. Others added pedals or longer strings. Some harpsichords were sixteen feet long!

Nothing really helped. The clavichord still played too softly, and the harpsichord was still too loud. What the musicians wanted was an instrument that could do both. The problem was solved, but not without some help from a very old instrument called the *dulcimer*.

PEDAL MANIA

Pedals for harpsichords became all the rage in the 1600's. Many harpsichords had pedals that would make sounds like bells, whistles, trumpets, even drums. Some harpsichords boasted as many as 25 pedals!

The Dulcimer

The dulcimer was invented about 2000 years ago in Persia. It had many strings and was played with a pair of "hammers" that looked like hefty drumsticks. When a hammer hit a string, a note sounded. Each string was stretched tight and tuned to a different note.

For hundreds of years, folks in the Western world did not know about this wonderful instrument. They went on plucking their monochords and playing their clavichords and harpsichords. They didn't discover the dulcimer until the early 1700's. The problem of loud and soft was about to be solved.

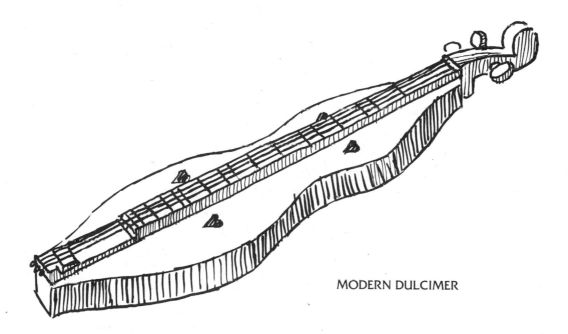

MODERN DULCIMER

The Pianoforte

In 1711, an Italian named Bartolomeo Cristofori invented a new instrument which he called the "loud-soft." In Italian, it came out *pianoforte*. By pressing a key gently, he could play softly. By hitting the key harder, he played loudly. Cristofori had solved the problem of loud and soft.

The simple dulcimer had helped him to do it. Instead of using quills, like the harpsichord, or brass strips, like the clavichord, Cristofori hit the strings with hammers. It was very much like the dulcimer, except that Cristofori had invented a set of fancy levers to send the hammers flying against the strings, much the way they do today.

But even the pianoforte had a problem. It wasn't very strong. The entire piano was made of wood, even the frame that held the tightly stretched strings. If a pianist played too hard, the strings would break with a terrible, dangerous TWANG!

THE GREAT STRING BUSTER

Franz Liszt, a very popular composer and pianist about 150 years ago, played his wood-frame pianos so hard that he often broke the strings. Liszt sometimes went through three pianos in just one concert!

SOME STRANGE PIANOS

Today's pianos come in two shapes: the graceful grand and the rectangular upright. Here are some of the shapes that you won't see around anymore.

GIRAFFE PIANO

OVAL PIANO

SQUARE PIANO

PYRAMIDAL PIANO

HARP PIANO

Today's Pianos

In today's pianos, an iron frame holds the piano strings tightly in place. Few pianists can break a piano string now. New glues, stronger wires, and hundreds of patented inventions make today's pianos stronger and easier to play.

Most of the best violins in the world today were made before the piano was even invented. No one has ever been able to match the quality of those old violins, but pianos are getting better and better. Piano companies improve their pianos in many ways every year.

Cristofori would not have believed it! Nor would he have believed how many different kinds of pianos have grown from his first one.

The Grand Pianos

Pianists who play for a living like the concert grand piano best. Its action is quick and it has a beautiful sound. The concert grand is still the biggest of all the grand pianos, but grands now come in smaller sizes.

THE SUPER-GRAND PIANO

The largest concert grand piano built today is made in Vienna by a company called Bösendorfer. This giant piano is 9½ feet long and has 9 more bass keys than a standard concert grand.

The biggest piano ever built was nearly three times heavier than today's big concert grand and measured 11 feet, 8 inches. It was made by Charles H. Challen and Sons in 1935.

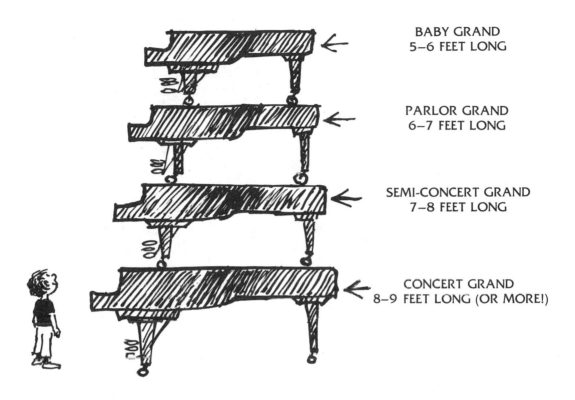

BABY GRAND
5–6 FEET LONG

PARLOR GRAND
6–7 FEET LONG

SEMI-CONCERT GRAND
7–8 FEET LONG

CONCERT GRAND
8–9 FEET LONG (OR MORE!)

PIANOS FALL APART!

Few instruments are stronger than the modern piano, but now and then, they play some terrible tricks on their pianists:

The pedals once fell off a piano that famous pianist André Watts was playing.

The bench once collapsed under pianist Bobby Short.

And while Myron Kropp was performing for a Russian audience, one of the piano's front legs broke!

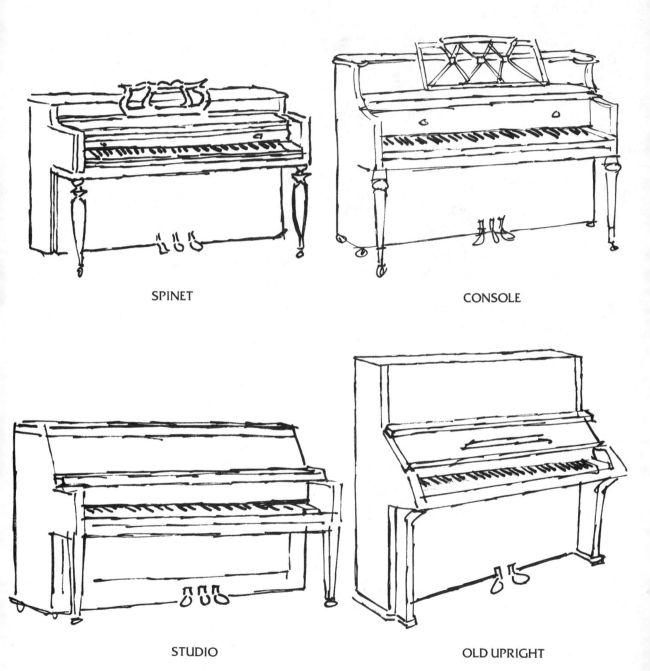

SPINET

CONSOLE

STUDIO

OLD UPRIGHT

The Upright Pianos

About 180 years ago, someone got an idea: instead of laying the piano strings out flat, stand them on end. The result was the upright piano, a piano that could be pushed near a wall.

Although the first upright pianos went up to the ceiling, they have become smaller and smaller. Today you can choose from sizes to fit nearly any house or apartment.

The upright made the piano more popular than ever. Pianos were now easier to build and cheaper to buy, and they fit into most homes. Millions of people have bought pianos and learned how to play them.

You may want to learn, too. The best time to learn to play the piano is when you are young. And the best time to start is now.

WE LOVE PIANOS

Japan produces more pianos than any other country in the world. Today, more pianos are made in Japan than in the United States and Russia combined.

A MOVING STORY

It takes at least three people to move a concert grand piano from one building to another. On the other hand, it's possible for just one person, using a special piano dolly, to move an upright piano.

How to Ride the Piano

Playing the piano is a lot like riding a bicycle. Like the bicycle, the piano is a good-sized piece of machinery. It takes your whole body to control it. You need your hands, your arms, your feet, your eyes, and your ears.

Hands

People who like to play the piano develop very strong hands. Surprisingly, you need muscle to play softly and fast. That kind of playing takes enormous control. Most pianists play exercises to build up the strength in their hands.

After you play a piece of music many times, it "gets into your hands." Your hands seem to know what to do without your thinking about it. It is much like tying your shoe. Once your hands learn how to make a bow, you can do it without even looking.

HOT AND COLD PIANO HANDS

Which hands play best—hot ones or cold? Pianists do not agree. Glenn Gould likes to soak his hands in hot water before a concert, to relax them. But other pianists put their hands in cold water, to wake them up.

People who play the piano for a living take very good care of their hands. All keep their fingernails short to keep them from clacking on the keys. Some pianists even have their hands insured.

HANDS ON!

You don't need big hands to play the piano. The size of your hands is not terribly important.

The hands of concert pianists differ enormously. Some have huge hands—Van Cliburn can span 12 white keys. Alicia de Larrocha has very small hands. She does stretching exercises to keep her fingers limber.

Some pianists have strangely shaped hands. Arthur Rubinstein's little finger was as long as his middle finger!

ONE-HANDED PIANO PIECE

When pianist Paul Wittgenstein lost his right arm in World War I, a famous composer named Maurice Ravel wrote a special piece of music for him. Ravel called it "Concerto for the Left Hand." Other famous pianists who have lost the use of their right hands have also performed this one-handed piece.

Feet

A piano has two (or three) pedals, and you need both feet to work them. Some piano players like to tap time with their feet while their fingers "tickle" the keys.

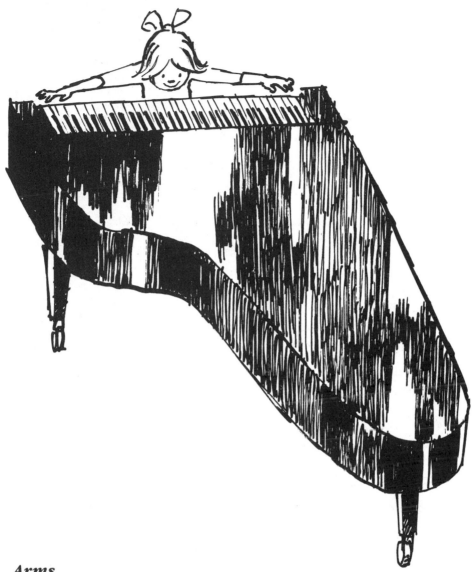

Arms

You can probably reach from one end of the keyboard to the other. The keyboard is built so that the person playing the piano can hit the top and bottom notes at the same time. If you can't do that yet, don't worry. You can still use your arms to give drama to the music you make with your fingers. Your arms help you play with power or as lightly as rain on the roof.

Ears

Most people begin playing the piano "by ear." They hear a tune and then try to pick it out on the piano. When it sounds right, they might add a few more notes to make it sound even better.

Many jazz pianists learned to play the piano this way. They taught themselves just by listening to music and trying to play what they heard.

Listening to someone else play is very important when you are learning to play the piano. You can listen to your parents or your friends, or you can listen to records or the radio. What goes into your ears can make those fingers MOVE!

IMPROVISE!

Jazz pianists love to improvise, which means that they make the music up as they play. You can have fun exploring the keyboard, too, making up little tunes. It's not much harder than talking!

LEARN BY LISTENING

The Suzuki method of teaching music became famous for training young violinists. Now there is also a Suzuki piano method. People who teach the Suzuki way believe that you can learn to play the piano the same way you learned to talk—by listening!

PRESIDENTIAL PIANOS

Every president of the United States but one has owned his own piano. Some, like Abraham Lincoln, even knew how to play it. President Truman was famous for his piano playing.

Eyes

You don't have to see to play the piano. Many fine pianists are blind. If you can see, however, you can learn to read music. Written music, called *music notation* or just plain *music*, tells you which notes to play and how fast to play them.

You learn to read music just as you learned to read these words. Instead of words, you read notes. Music uses a kind of picture language, which works for anyone from any country. Most Western music is written in the same musical "language."

There are some words, which give extra directions for playing the music. The words are usually in Italian, because it was the Italians who were the first to develop music notation. You already know two of those words—*forte* and *piano* (meaning loud and soft).

MUSICAL BRAILLE

You probably thought that Braille was invented to help people who can't see read books. Not so! Louis Braille first invented his system of raised bumps as a way for the blind to read music. Only later was it also used for words.

Feeling

Playing the piano is not entirely like riding a bike, of course. To play the piano well, you need to use your feelings. You have to love your piano and the music you can make on it.

The Piano Keyboard and How It Grew

Cristofori's keyboard had only 55 keys. Musicians complained that it wasn't enough, so bigger and bigger pianos were built. Today's keyboards have 88 keys.

Name That Note!

When you look at the keyboard, you will see a pattern. Each block of the pattern is made of 7 white keys and 5 black keys. There are seven complete sets of these patterns on the piano. The white keys are named with letters of the alphabet (A-B-C-D-E-F-G). The space between the first key of one pattern and the first key of the next is called an *octave*.

So the notes are not really as difficult as they look. They are just the same twelve tones, repeated at higher and lower places on the piano.

BIG BIRTHDAY

Our musical language will soon be 1000 years old! A monk named Guido d'Arezzo first used those five parallel lines and named the notes to put on them sometime around 1000 A.D.

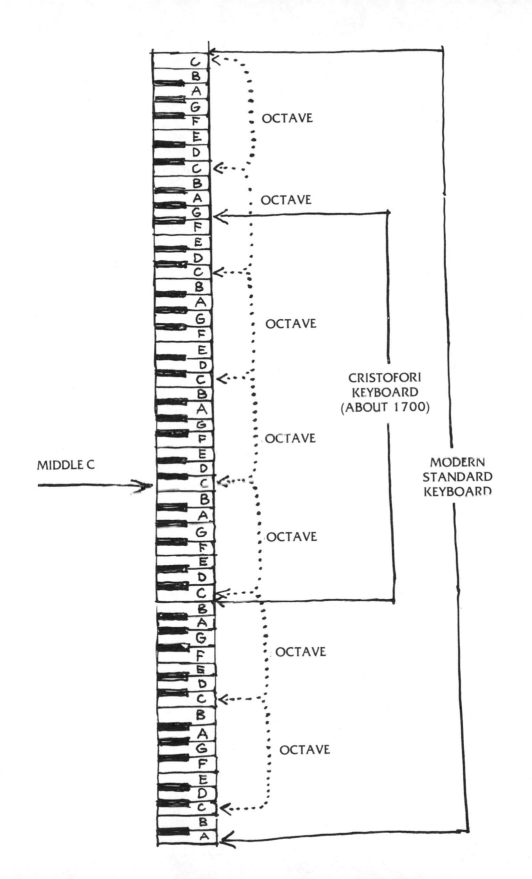

OCTAVE

OCTAVE

OCTAVE

OCTAVE

OCTAVE

OCTAVE

OCTAVE

OCTAVE

CRISTOFORI
KEYBOARD
(ABOUT 1700)

MODERN
STANDARD
KEYBOARD

MIDDLE C

All keyboards are created equal (almost)

The piano isn't the only instrument with a keyboard. Lots of other instruments have keyboards, too. And guess what? Those keyboards are all arranged the same way.

So if you can play the piano, you can quickly learn to play one of these nifty instruments—

The harpsichord. Believe it or not, the harpsichord is still around, looking much as it did 300 years ago. Some wonderful music was written for the harpsichord, so many people become expert harpsichordists.

The electric piano. Rock bands like the electric piano. It's portable—it has a very short keyboard—and its sound is amplified electrically into speakers much like a stereo's.

The organ. There are several kinds of organs, but most home organs are electric. Organs often have two keyboards as well as foot pedals for the really deep notes.

The accordion. For a truly portable keyboard, hang an accordion around your neck. You play the tune on the small keyboard at one end while pushing chord buttons at the other end. While you play, squeeze both ends together to make a cheerful sound.

The electronic keyboard. Want a trumpet, guitar, drums, piano, and goodness knows what else all rolled into one? Some kinds of electronic keyboards can give you more than a dozen different instruments' sounds, a built-in rhythm section, and even some whiz-bang cartoon sounds. If your electronic keyboard also has a computer—or a synthesizer—you can combine the sounds and turn yourself into an amazing, one-kid band!

Switching from a piano to another keyboard instrument is much like moving from a typewriter to a computer. The keyboards are so similar that, with a little extra effort, you can feel at home on both.

PIANOS THAT PLAY BY THEMSELVES

Some pianos—called player pianos—work like giant music boxes. A roll of paper with holes punched in it tells the piano keys what to play. Ragtime is the most popular kind of music on piano rolls.

AUTHORS CAN PLAY!

When E.B. White, author of *Charlotte's Web*, was a boy, his father worked for a piano company. The boy loved to visit his father at work and soon learned to play the piano he heard so often.

Paula Fox studied piano at the famous Juilliard School of Music before she began writing books for children.

AWFUL MUSIC

Many people think that "Chopsticks" is the worst piece of music ever written. They are outnumbered, though, by the people who like it. "Chopsticks," first published in 1877, has been popular for more than 100 years.

DO YOU COMPUTE?

If you have a computer, you may be able to buy computer programs that will help you learn to read and write music!

WE PLAY TOO!

You don't have to be a musician to play the piano. The author, the illustrator, and one of the editors for this book have all taken piano lessons. We still enjoy playing the piano.

SUPERMAN CAN!

When Superman is played by Christopher Reeve, he can play the piano very well. Actor Reeve says he practices the piano for 1 ½ hours every day.

MR. PIANO

Piano collector and author Bob Pierce loves pianos so much that he works at a piano-shaped desk, smokes a piano-shaped pipe, and claims to have the biggest collection of piano stickers in the world.

So What Are You Waiting For?

You can start playing the piano right now, if you have one. Try to pick out a simple tune that you know well. When you get that right, try another one. Listen to the radio and recordings of music that you like. Then see if you can play some of those tunes on the piano. Many people learn best "by ear," and that might be a good way for you, too.

Taking piano lessons is another way to learn. To find a good teacher, ask a friend who plays the piano well to suggest someone. Or contact one of the places suggested below.

Whichever way you choose to learn, keep playing. Practice makes progress!

Who Knows About Piano Teachers?

Your Chamber of Commerce
 Ask about music organizations in your area.

The music department of a local college or university
 One of the piano instructors might recommend a good teacher.

Piano and music stores

The National Guild of Piano Teachers
Box 1807
Austin, TX 78767

The Music Teachers National Association
2113 Carew Tower
Cincinnati, OH 45202

Be Kind to Your Piano

If you are lucky enough to own a piano, here are some nice things you can do for it:

1. Take good care of your piano. Wipe the dust off the keys with a damp cloth. (Don't use a wet one—water might drip between the keys. Because water makes wood swell, the keys might stick.)

2. Make sure your piano gets a tune-up twice a year. You can find a piano tuner listed in the Yellow Pages, or ask a musician to recommend one. Piano tuners make house-calls, so you can watch your tuner take your own piano apart. Most tuners are happy to show you the parts of the piano. Yours will be impressed with how much you know.

3. Hug your piano once in a while. It may be a machine, but it has its own personality. No two pianos sound exactly the same.

4. Most important, play your piano. You can play any kind of music on a piano—rock, jazz, ragtime, blues, classical music, or popular songs. You may even want to become a musician when you grow up. You don't have to do that to enjoy the piano, though. What you learn now will stay with you all of your life.

Making music is a great way to spend time at any age.

No matter how impressive the piano seems, by itself it is just a machine. It needs someone like you to turn it into much more than that—a marvelous musical *instrument*!